Tales from Toadstool Glade

Wally's Party

written by Louise Warnes

Illustration by Becky Morgan

AuthorHouse™ UK
1663 Liberty Drive
Bloomington, IN 47403 USA
www.authorhouse.co.uk
UK TFN: 0800 0148641 (Toll Free inside the UK)
UK Local: 02036 956322 (+44 20 3695 6322 from outside the UK)

Because of the dynamic nature of the Internet, any web addresses or links contained in this book may have changed
since publication and may no longer be valid. The views expressed in this work are solely those of the author and do
not necessarily reflect the views of the publisher, and the publisher hereby disclaims any responsibility for them.

Any people depicted in stock imagery provided by Getty Images are models,
and such images are being used for illustrative purposes only.
Certain stock imagery © Getty Images.

This book is printed on acid-free paper.

ISBN: 979-8-8230-8136-8 (sc)
ISBN: 979-8-8230-8135-1 (e)

Print information available on the last page.

Published by AuthorHouse 03/24/2023

authorHOUSE

Now, as you may know, worms are exceedingly small. And Wally was an exceedingly small worm. He was shy, and because he thought other animals would laugh at him, he didn't really mix with anyone. He kept himself to himself.

So he was not an incredibly happy worm. He really wanted to make some friends he could spend time with and have some fun with.

Belinda Butterfly was a very friendly lady, and as she was flitting between some pretty flowers, she happened to see Wally looking very forlorn and sad.

"Good morning, my friend! Why are you looking so unhappy?" she asked.

Wally looked up and said, "I would so like to have someone to be my friend. In fact, I would like more than one friend! But I am too shy to go and say hello to all the different animals that pass by, and they never notice me because I am so small and not interesting."

"Oh dear, that's too bad," answered Belinda. "We need to do something about this!"

Belinda fluttered down and stood by Wally. "I think the best way to meet new friends is to have a party."

"A party!" exclaimed Wally. He couldn't think of anything worse than a party—especially if it was his party! He wouldn't be able to hide, and he knew others would laugh at him for being an exceedingly small worm.

"Yes, a party," said Belinda. "And I will help you arrange it. I love parties!"

"Well, okay," replied Wally. "If you think anyone will want to come."

Belinda flitted around excitedly. "I know so many lovely animals who would love to come and meet you. There's the Snail family. Maisie Mouse is extremely sweet. Prickles and Penny are hedgehogs—oh, don't look so alarmed," she said to Wally, who had turned quite pale at the word *hedgehogs*. "They won't eat you—I promise! You will have a lot in common with Murphy Mole; he is a very quiet and shy sort of mole, but so friendly once you get to know him.

"Let me think who else we could invite. Oh yes, Tilly and Tony Tortoise—they are so easy to get on with and never ever in a hurry. Ron and Rita, the two rabbits, don't hang around too long; they always seem to have somewhere to hop off to."

Wally listened to Belinda; he already felt she was his friend and was beginning to feel a little bit excited.

"How can we let them know there is going to be a party?" he asked.

"We send out invitations, of course," replied Belinda, "once we have decided where we are going to hold your party."

Wally and Belinda thought long and hard about where to hold the party.

"How about in Toadstool Glade? The toadstools make very nice seats," said Belinda.

"Yes, that's a very good idea," said Wally, who by now had wiggled right out of his hole in the ground and forgotten about hiding away.

They decided they would write the invitations on the leaves that were beneath the tall oak tree nearby. Belinda collected them one at a time, and with a very thin twig in his mouth, Wally wrote on them:

Please Come to My Party
in Toadstool Glade
2:00 p.m.
Love,
Wally

On a nearby bush, Bishy and Barnaby the ladybirds were listening to Wally and Belinda.

"Do you think they will ask us?" Bishy whispered to Barnaby.

"Why don't we go and say hello now?" said Barnaby. So they flew over and landed on a blade of grass near Wally.

"Excuse us for butting in, but we heard you are having a party, and we would love to be invited."

Wally and Belinda looked at the two little ladybirds.

"Of course you can come," exclaimed Wally. "You are very welcome!"

Now hiding behind a large bush was someone who was not happy. And because he was not happy, he didn't like seeing others happy either.

Cedric Caterpillar was feeling cross; in fact he felt very grumpy. He didn't like the way he looked, he didn't like the way he felt inside, and he didn't want anyone else to feel happy.

So as he listened to the plans for Wally's party, he was thinking of a plan to spoil it.

"I am going to find every invitation and eat it," he said, "because I am certain I will not be invited."

Poor Cedric—he really was a very unhappy caterpillar.

Meanwhile, Wally and Belinda now had the help of Bishy and Barnaby to write the invitations. It took a while, as Wally was not very quick at writing. But by the time the sun was setting, between the four friends, they had managed to get a pile of invitations ready to be delivered first thing the next morning.

Please come
to my Party
At Toadstool
Glade
at 2pm
Love
Wally
X

They put the invitations in a safe place, under a stone beside Wally's hole, so the wind would not blow them away. Then the four friends all went home feeling extremely excited, especially Wally.

Very early the next morning, Cedric made his way to the pile of leaves under the stone. Some of the leaves were poking out, so he started to nibble at them one by one. As he nibbled, the stone started to move, and the leafy invitations were uncovered. Before long all that was left were little bits of leaves and no invitations.

Wally Worm woke up feeling so much happier than he had ever felt before. He quickly made his way up through his tunnel and popped his head out into the early-morning sunshine just as Belinda arrived.

But Belinda saw at once something was very wrong. "Wally," she said, "have you delivered the invitations already?"

"Oh no, Belinda, I have to leave that job to you," replied Wally.

"So where are they?" asked Belinda, beginning to feel very anxious.

Wally looked at where they had been left under the stone, but they were all gone!

"I don't know!" he cried. "I don't know where they have gone."

Poor Wally and Belinda! After all their hard work getting them ready to deliver, all the invitations were no longer there.

Wally looked so downcast, and Belinda, who was naturally a happy butterfly, was looking very upset.

Who or what could have taken the invitations?

As they sat wondering what to do, Bishy and Barnaby flew down.

"We have come to help give out the invitations," they said excitedly. Then they noticed their two friends looking sad.

Then Belinda said in a quiet voice, "Someone or something has taken them away."

Sure enough, where the invitations had been left under the stone, there were just a few bits of leaf.

Well, the four friends were quiet for a while, all thinking what to do. Then they all heard a very strange sound; it seemed to be coming from some bushes behind them.

"Can you hear that strange noise?" asked Bishy. It started quietly, then got louder and louder, and then went softer again.

"Yes, I can hear it," said Wally.

"So can I," replied Belinda and Barnaby.

Very quietly, Belinda flew up over the bush to see if there was anything to see.

There, lying fast asleep, was a very bloated caterpillar, snoring very loudly.

Belinda flew back down to her friends. "It's that grumpy caterpillar Cedric, and I have a nasty feeling he may have been the one who ate the invitations."

"Well, what can we do?" wailed Wally. "I was looking so forward to my party, and now we don't have any invitations to give out."

Bishy and Barnaby were looking glum too, but Belinda had a determined look on her face. "You shall have your party, Wally. Instead of giving out invitations, I will go and invite everyone I know myself. I can fly quickly, and I will tell everyone to pass it on to their friends. I will tell them all to bring their favourite food and drink. So I had better start right this minute!"

With that Belinda fluttered her large, beautiful wings and was gone.

Wally sat with Bishy and Barnaby. "I don't think Belinda will be able to make Murphy Mole hear her; I think I will go and knock on his cellar door." And with that Wally dived down his hole to wake Murphy up.

Bishy and Barnaby looked at each other. "How could Cedric be so horrid, eating all those invitations?" murmured Bishy.

"Well, I hope he is sick," retorted Barnaby. "He certainly doesn't deserve to go to the party."

"No, I agree; he is so grumpy," said Bishy.

They sat silent for a while. Then Bishy said, "I wonder what makes him so grumpy and cross."

"I guess he just isn't happy inside," replied Barnaby.

"The trouble is," said Bishy, "no one likes a grumpy, cross caterpillar, so no one wants to be his friend. And that would make him sadder, grumpier and even more cross."

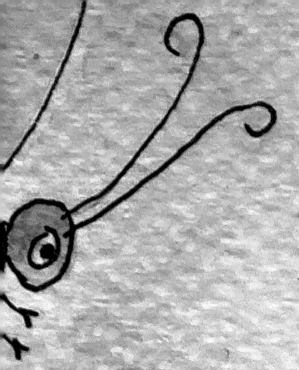

Just then Wally returned. "I managed to wake Murphy up. My, it took a lot of banging to make him hear! But he says he would love to come to my party."

Suddenly the noise from the bush behind them started to get even louder, and they could hear groans. The two ladybirds flew up to see, and there was poor Cedric, looking very ill and obviously feeling very sick.

Cedric looked at them through blurry eyes and tried to say something nasty, but he felt too ill.

They flew back down to Wally and told him about Cedric and how poorly and ill he looked. "Well, I expect eating all those leaves must have given him an awful stomach ache," said Wally.

"Yes, it will make him even grumpier and more cross," said Bishy.

Wally was very kind-hearted; he knew what it was like to feel sad and lonely, and he kind of felt sorry for Cedric, even though he had eaten all the invitations. "Bishy and Barnaby, could you ask Cedric whether he would like to come to my party please?"

"What if he doesn't want to or says something nasty to us?" asked Barnaby.

"Just say he is still welcome, and we hope he soon feels better."

So the two ladybirds flew back to where Cedric was now sitting up and looking sorry for himself. Before they could say anything, he said, "Okay, don't keep coming and laughing at me; just go away!"

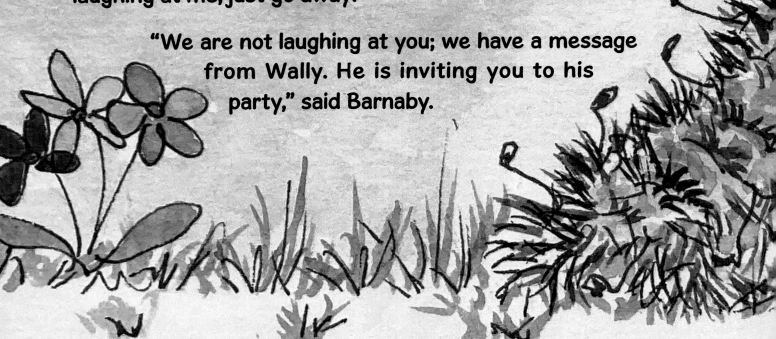

"We are not laughing at you; we have a message from Wally. He is inviting you to his party," said Barnaby.

Cedric looked taken aback. Was he hearing them right? After he had eaten all the invitations out of spite and nastiness, Wally still asked him to come to the party. "Why would Wally want me at his party after I ate all the invitations?" he asked.

"Because," said Bishy, "Wally is a very kind and generous worm."

Cedric started to make his way slowly down from the bush to the ground, where Wally was waiting for the ladybirds to come back.

Cedric still felt extremely uncomfortable, and he was also feeling something else: he felt ashamed and sorry for what he had done.

"Wally, I am so sorry for eating your invitations. I heard you talking about your party and who was going to be invited, but I didn't hear my name. So I wanted to spoil things."

Wally looked at Cedric. "I would have asked you, but you always seem so cross and grumpy. I am very shy and not very brave, so I felt a bit scared of you. I think we are both a bit the same. I hide away and keep quiet because I don't think others will want to be my friend, and you feel the same but act cross and grumpy to hide how you feel."

Cedric and Wally looked at each other and suddenly felt they had each found a friend, one who understood them.

As Wally, Cedric, Bishy, and Barnaby were sitting quietly, Belinda suddenly flew over them and came and stood beside them.

"Phew, I am so exhausted. I have flown everywhere, and everyone I have asked is coming!" Then she saw Cedric sitting beside Wally.

"What is he doing here?" she exclaimed. "How can you have him sit beside you after all he has done?"

Wally sighed. He knew Belinda had a right to be cross, seeing Cedric sitting there while she had been flying all over the place. Wally didn't want to fall out with Belinda, but he had to make her see why Cedric had done what he did.

Slowly Cedric started to make his way back to his bush, but Wally stopped him. "Cedric, don't go. I am going to explain to Belinda why I want you to come to my party."

"He is coming to your party!" spluttered Belinda, sounding even more outraged.

"Yes he is, and I am showing him true friendship, just like you showed me when I was feeling so sad and unloved and unnoticed. You were my first friend, Belinda, and my very special friend, so now I am passing that on and being a friend to Cedric. I know he was wrong to eat our invitations, and he did do it out of spite. But it was because he was feeling sad, cross, grumpy, and unloved."

Wally had never said so much in one go before and sat rather out of breath, hoping Belinda would stop being cross and understand.

Belinda looked at Wally. "You know, Wally, for such a small, shy worm, you have an enormous heart." She then looked at Cedric and said, "Wally has shown great kindness to you, so, Cedric, I forgive you too."

With that, Wally, Belinda, Bishy, Barnaby, and Cedric started to make their way to Toadstool Glade for the party.

Wally felt very excited! He had already made four friends, and he was looking forward to making more new friends at his party.

Suddenly, out of nowhere, two furry rabbits rushed past, stopped, bumped into each other, and turned round,

"Ron and Rita!" exclaimed Belinda. "Stop and meet Wally."

The two rabbits hopped towards Wally. "Hello, Wally! Thank you so much for inviting us to your party; we love parties—don't we, Ron?" said Rita, who was holding a bag of juicy carrots and lettuce. "We don't want to be late, so we had better hurry. See you soon!" And off they hopped at great speed.

Belinda laughed. "They will have to wait till we arrive before the party can begin."

They had not gone very far when Wally stopped and listened. "What's that funny noise?" he asked.

They all stopped and listened. Sure enough, there was a very slow plodding sound. Coming through the long grass were two tortoises. Bishy and Barnaby flew down and landed on their backs. "Tilly and Tony, it's so good to see you!" said Barnaby. "We love having a ride on your shells."

"You are always very welcome—aren't they, Tony?" said Tilly.

"Oh yes!" said Tony.

Tilly turned very slowly toward, Wally who was fascinated by the two tortoises. "And thank you so much for inviting us to your party, Wally. It is most kind. Come on, Tony. We must keep going; otherwise we won't get to the party!"

Wally, Belinda, and Cedric soon overtook Tony and Tilly; Bishy and Barnaby were still having a ride on their hard shells. "See you soon!" they called to the three friends as they plodded slowly along.

They soon left Tony and Tilly behind. Wally and Cedric wished they had wings like Belinda. It was hard work slithering along the ground.

All of a sudden, the ground in front of them seemed to start to move. A big pile of earth appeared, and out of the top of the mound popped a furry black head with whiskers and a long wiggly nose.

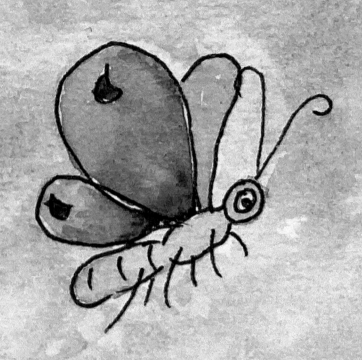

"Oh, Murphy!" exclaimed Wally. "You gave us quite a fright. How lovely to see you!"

"Oh dear," said Murphy. "I do apologise. I thought I had reached the Toadstool Glade, but I have a little farther to go. I will see you at the party. Goodbye!" And with that he disappeared again, leaving Wally and Cedric to go around the mound of earth.

Belinda, who was flying just in front of Wally and Cedric, called, "We are there! I can see all the toadstools." And sure enough, as the two friends hurried up a little hill, there in front of them was Toadstool Glade.

It was such a pretty place. Flowers grew between the toadstools, and tall, slender trees kept it shaded from the sun.

As Wally reached a shady place to cool down, a little voice from above him said, "Hello, Wally! Thank you so much for asking us to your party."

Wally looked up and saw three snails sitting on a large toadstool.

"I am Shelly," said the largest one, "and these two are Silvee and Slow-mo."

"It's so kind of you to come," replied Wally. "I didn't think anyone would be interested in coming to my party."

"Oh, we love parties, and we don't get asked to many," replied Silvee, "so thank you!"

In the centre of the toadstools was one very large flat one, like a table. As the party guests arrived, they gave their food to a very small fieldmouse, who quickly set it out on the table. She was here, there, and everywhere, making sure everything was just how she liked it.

Belinda called to her: "Maisie, come here and meet Wally, our party boy!"

Maisie hurried over. "Wally, how lovely to meet you; thank you for inviting me! I do love parties." She nodded at the table. "I am making sure everyone puts the food together."

"You are doing a very good job, Maisie," said Belinda.

As Wally looked around, he could see Murphy had put up a large mound of earth and was looking around. He had his glasses on, as he was extremely short-sighted.

Two very prickly hedgehogs came ambling up to where Wally and Cedric were sitting. "You must be Wally," one of the hedgehogs said.

"Yes, I am Wally, and this is Cedric," replied Wally.

"I am Prickles, and this is Penny. We are so happy you asked us to your party; thank you so much!"

Wally beamed; he was suddenly feeling very warm and happy inside. "No, I must thank you for coming. I didn't think anyone would want to come, and now look!"

Wally watched as the tortoises came ambling into the glade. Ron and Rita were hopping around very excitedly, the ladybirds were flitting about, and Murphy was peering around at all that was going on. The snails were chatting to Belinda. But when he looked to where Cedric had been, he was not there!

"Belinda!" called Wally. "Cedric has gone; he has disappeared."

Belinda flew down to Wally. "Well, he said he still wasn't feeling very well; maybe he is just having a quick rest. Don't worry; I will keep an eye out for him. I am sure he is fine."

Wally, who had grown to like Cedric, hoped Belinda was right. He went to sit in a special place Maisie had made for him in the middle of the glade.

As more and more guests arrived, the glade was filled with lots of happy sounds. Everyone said hello to Wally and added their food to the table. Shelly, Silvee, and Slo-mo the snails perched on the toadstools, and Tony and Tilly Tortoise stopped under the shade of an extra-large one. Walking to the glade had tired them out, but they were so pleased to be amongst so many friends.

Prickles and Penny the hedgehogs were chatting to Murphy Mole, and Ron and Rita were helping Maisie to set the food out in a tidy manner on the large flat toadstool. But they were causing more mayhem because they were so quick at everything.

As the sun shone through the leafy branches of the tall, slender trees, Belinda picked a bluebell and rang it. The guests stopped what they were doing and looked to where she hovered in the air above them.

"Listen, everyone!" she called. "I would like to welcome you all to Wally's party. Yesterday he was feeling sad, lonely, and unloved, so I promised him I would find him some friends by having a party. And now here you all are! Wally, here are your friends; you need never feel lonely again."

Wally was feeling overwhelmed with happiness. "Thank you so much, Belinda, for arranging this party! I cannot believe how many of you wanted to come, as I am just an ordinary and dull little worm. But you have made me feel so happy, and I love you all."

With that a big cheer went up from all those gathered in the glade. "Hip hip hooray for Wally!" shouted Ron the rabbit.

Then everyone yelled, "Hooray for Wally!"

Then the guests started to eat the food they had brought, and Maisie Mouse went round with some cold spring water in little acorn cups.

By the time the sun had slid low behind the trees, all the animals felt full and contented. They chatted together with Wally in the centre of the ring of toadstools.

Soon it was time to say goodnight to one another, Ron and Rita hopped away, although not so quickly, as they were full of carrots! Prickles and Penny simply curled up underneath a nearby bush. The three snails disappeared inside their shells, and Murphy found his mound of earth and burrowed back down into his tunnel to go back home. Maisie scampered off into the nearby field, back to her home. Belinda, Bishy, Barnaby, and Wally waved goodbye to all of them and then started to go back to Wally's home.

"Thank you so much, Belinda," said Wally, yawning before slipping into his hole. "And you, Bishy and Barnaby/ I feel so different inside! It's a lovely warm, fuzzy feeling. I have so many good friends and all because of you being so kind."

Belinda and the two ladybirds smiled. Belinda said, "You are very welcome; after all we all need to feel loved and wanted, and being kind to one another is the most important thing to be."

Wally suddenly looked sad. "I do feel a little worried about Cedric, though. I hope he feels better; I missed him at the party."

"We will go and find him tomorrow," replied Belinda. "Don't worry, Wally; I am sure he will be feeling much better by the morning."

They all said good night and went to settle down for the night.

Wally went to bed feeling loved and happy knowing he need never be lonely again.

Printed in the United States
by Baker & Taylor Publisher Services